Sam Benjamin and Candice Lori's

The

Hippie

Kama

Sutra

A special thanks to *People of the Rainbow: A Nomadic Utopia*, by Michael I. Niman, and *The Smell Report* from the Social Issues Research Center.

Sam Benjamin and Candice Lori's

The Hippie Kama Sutra

With Illustrations by Sam Wohl

Rare Bird Books | Los Angeles, Calif.

THIS IS A GENUINE RARE BIRD BOOK

A Rare Bird Book | Rare Bird Books
453 South Spring Street, Suite 531
Los Angeles, CA 90013
rarebirdbooks.com

FIRST HARDCOVER EDITION

Set in Lato
Printed in the United States
Distributed in the US by Publishers Group West

10 9 8 7 6 5 4 3 2 1

Publisher's Cataloging-in-Publication data

Benjamin, Sam.
  Hippie Kama sutra / by Sam Benjamin and Candice Lori ; illustrations by Sam Wohl.
  p.cm.
  ISBN 978-1-940207-28-5

1. Sex. 2. Love. 3. Sexual intercourse. 4. Hippies. 5. Marijuana. 6. Cannabis. 7. Subculture. I. Lori, Candice. II. Wohl, Sam. III. Title.

HQ31 .B46 2014
306.7—dc23

This book is dedicated to the Lover, the Earth Steward, and the Freak in you.

Sam Benjamin
&
Candice Lori ♡

INTRODUCTION

Hippies are incredibly sexy. We've always thought that.

Sure, we know: To the uninitiated, the average Hippie may be a bit rough around the edges. But to their hard-core devotees, these hairy, peace-loving, armpit-stanking, cannabis-puffing, beautiful-smile-having, free-spirited folk possess spectacular appeal.

Everyone's fallen for a hippie at least once. Remember that dude with the waist-long dreads, who you met at The Other Ones show back in '99—the one who convinced you to help him ship twenty pounds of ganja back to the Midwest, smuggled in hula hoops?

Or that babe at the retreat center, the one who made her own herbal tinctures, her own deodorant, and her own beeswax votive candles—the one who warned you on your first meeting, "Listen, I don't normally vibe well romantically with water signs—but if you're a Capricorn, we can get funky..."

Hippies are hard to forget, and nearly impossible not to love. They follow their passions unapologetically: community, pleasure, laughter, music, the wisdom of the Earth. Superfoods, sunshine, and spreading love are the top priorities of the day.

We were inspired to create this book by our own experiences living amongst the unique tribe that we love, admire, and draw inspiration from, as well as our shared passion for living the sexiest, healthiest, most dynamic life possible.

This is no ordinary sex book. This is actually a guidebook for better living. Sex is merely the vehicle of delivery, because it's so gosh darn fun and makes for some great illustrations.

We hope you laugh, we hope you learn from the wisdom of the hippie way, and we hope that you even get a little turned on in the process and take some of that juiciness back into your own life.

Our *Hippie Kama Sutra*, in a nutshell: Love and respect yourself, each other, and mama Earth.

—SAM AND CANDICE

"If God dropped acid, would he see people?"
—Steven Wright

Mexican mango, monukka raisins, golden flax seeds, wild jungle peanuts, Sri Lankan red rice, the ever-present goji berry. Bursting with micronutrients and thrillingly high in fiber, these expensive edibles can be found down at the local bulk bin, where hippies meet and mingle, scrawling four-digit codes on twist ties as they surreptitiously dip their nimble fingers into the superfood granola bin for a quick nibble. Under the radiant glow of supermarket lights, a gentle smile, a shy moment of eye contact, and a double handful of nutritional yeast can go a long way.

APHRODISIAFACT:

Magnesium has documented aphrodisiac effects that include increasing your libido and improving sexual performance. It is also crucial in production of healthy sperm and eggs. What are you waiting for? Get on over to the local health food store and look for some of these magnesium-rich seeds, nuts, and sexy spices in the bulk food section: squash seeds, flax seeds, sesame seeds, tahini, dried coriander, dill, sage, basil, cocoa powder, molasses, brown rice, rice bran, and wheat germ.

HIGH-MAGNESIUM HAPPY TRAIL MIX:
PUMPKIN SEEDS
SUNFLOWER SEEDS
BRAZIL NUTS
ALMONDS
CASHEWS
CACAO NIBS

THE HIPPIE KAMA SUTRA'S TOP 5 HEALTH FOOD STORE PICK-UP LINES:

- "Do you believe in love at first sight, or should I walk by again?"
- "You know what's on the menu tonight? Me 'n' you."
- "Do you like strawberries or blueberries? 'Cause I need to know what pancakes to make you in the morning."
- "Baby you remind me of my spice cabinet, 'cause you got a fine grind goin' on."
- "You're my missing ingredient."

"For it is in giving that we receive."
    —St. Francis of Assisi

*W*hat's more of a turn-on than wrapping your lips around a bar of organic dark chocolate with spicy chilies, whetting your palate with a steamy cup of fresh-roasted Guatemalan coffee, or lubing up your body with some organic whole virgin coconut oil? There is no higher ideal for the hippie than indulging the senses with a clear conscience. These awakened ones strive to create partnerships based on reciprocity, empowerment, and sustainability—where everyone wins! Thinking globally, acting locally may rock your world.

AND THE SURVEY SAYS...

Researchers from the National Survey of Sexual Health and Behavior surveyed ,865 people aged fourteen to ninety-four, finding that contrary to popular belief, men, specially as they get older, give as much oral sex to women as women give to men!

The greatest disparity is in the twenty to twenty-four year range, with fifty-ve percent of men saying they've given it in the past year, compared to seventy-our percent of women. The tables turn as they age, with sixty-nine percent coincidentally) of men in the thirty to thirty-nine age range reporting giving oral ex, and only fifty-nine percent of women doing the same.

FAIRPLAY:

The French Letter Condom Company offers guilt-free condoms to the citizens f the world who want to feel good in every way when they make love. The condoms re manufactured in Germany from natural latex harvested under sustainable and ertified Fair Trade conditions.

The term "French Letter" comes from English seventeenth century tourists who tumbled across the French town of Condom, where the French shepherds were naking prophylactics from sheep gut. Trade between the English and French ensued, nd the English would anxiously await the letters from France—the French Letters, ull of a fresh batch of condoms.

FAIRBOOTY:

Pants to Poverty is a British company (in England pants are not trousers, they're underwear) that aims to provide underwear for all people, in a way that supports and espects the humans that make them, including their Indian farmers and factory workers.

THE DOUBLE D

EADLOCK

Dreads have been revered throughout history and across innumerable cultures; their devotees including Kenyan Maasai warriors, Hindu Sadhus, Pre-Colombian Aztec priests, Jamaican Rastas, Nazarite Jews, and Tibetan-Buddhist Ngagpas. Dread love goes as far back as Ancient Egypt— mummies unearthed on archaelogical digs have had locks!

Dreads are mystical, endowed with cryptic energies: When activated and blessed, they may serve as antennae to intergalatic communiqués. Dreads look sweet on a dance floor and feel smart bound up in a knit cap. Whether adorned with crystals, dyed magenta in a fit of whimsy, or wrapped around your lover's hand, they are the hippie gift that keeps on giving.

CRIMES OF THE HAIR

In 2013, the *Johannesburg Times Live* reported that in South Africa, criminals have increasingly been preying upon unwitting clubgoers and travelers with dreadlocks, chopping off their hair and then selling the locks to hair salons who use them as extensions. One such victim, Zimbabwean Mutsa Madonko, was at a nightclub when he passed out briefly. When he woke up, he still had his wallet and phone, but his dreads were gone. Reportedly, a long set of dreadlocks can fetch up to $300 on the Johannesburg black market.

SLOW YOUR ROLL:
TOP 8 DREAD SHORTCUTS TO AVOID

We know, the promise of Rasta locks is pretty darn enticing, and you're willing to take some chances! But please, avoid starting your dread experience with . . .

MUD
CHEWING GUM
CANDLEWAX
PEANUT BUTTER
MAYONNAISE
RUBBER CEMENT
TOOTHPASTE

(or those little rubber bands that you get from the orthodontist)
Alas, there is no known shortcut to the holy dreadlock.
Only time and rasta effort can get you there.

"No matter how little money and how few possessions you own, having a dog makes you feel rich."

—Louis Sabin

*I*nside the happiest hippie households, there's a special place reserved for the warm, wagging tongue of the family dog. *Canis lupus hippius*—an extraordinarily loyal, playful species that includes all manner of mutt, mongrel, and mixed-breed—may never take Best in Show, but these lovable pack animals will win you over with their limitless reserves of earnestness and devotion. Like their owners, they're drawn to the simpler things in life: a warm bed, a good head rub, and a friendship that can last a lifetime.

Did You Know?

Dogs hear far more acutely than humans, recognizing noises up to four times farther away than those that humans can detect.

However, they aren't as subtle when it comes to taste. Dogs have 1,700 tastebuds compared to humans' 9,000. Cats have even fewer, at 473.

Each dog has a dominant paw. They are right-pawed or left-pawed, like humans are right-handed or left-handed.

Dogs' nose prints are as unique as human fingerprints and can be used to identify them.

Touch is crucial to dogs. Their entire bodies, including paws, are covered with touch-sensitive nerve endings. Give a dog a massage!

Petting dogs has been shown to lower the blood pressure of their owners. Playing with dogs can elevate levels of serotonin and dopamine, which wards off depression.

Reportedly, the best dog to help you get romantic attention is a golden retriever. The worst is a pit bull.

You might not always want to give a big smile to a dog that you are meeting for the first time. He or she may interpret your bared teeth as an act of agression.

Male dogs raise their legs when they urinate on a tree in order to aim higher, in an attempt send the territorial message that they are taller and bigger than they are. Some wild dogs in Africa run up tree trunks as they urinate, to appear very large.

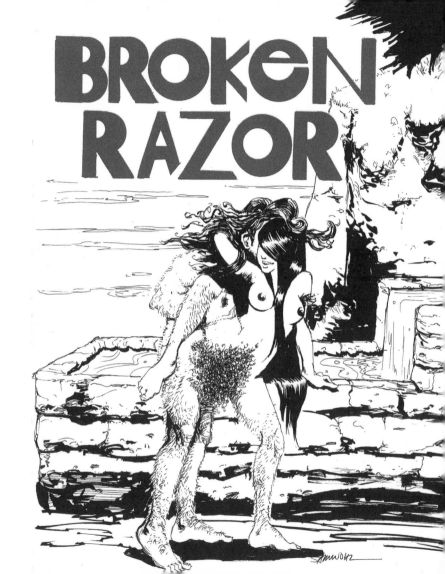

Primitive man was a bushy beast: thick-bearded, well-pubed. Original woman, too, sported a sensual shag—her power-goddess bursting forth, unadulterated, aromatic, sexy as hell. Today's hirsute hippie is a throwback to stubblier times: a furry noncomforist, bewhiskered, blissed-out, reveling in the surprising joy of natural, unshorn beauty.

A Brief History of Shaving

Underarms: Before 1915, American women rarely shaved their underarms. Then sleeveless dresses became popular—and an advertisement in *Harper's Bazaar* strongly recommended "the removal of objectionable hair." In 1922, the first women's razors showed up in the Sears Roebuck catalog, and by the mid-1920s, hairy underarms were a fashion no-no.

Legs: Before 1940, few women saw the point in shaving their legs. But with shorter skirts, sheer stockings, and the emergence of pin-up queen Betty Grable, American women in the post-WWII era suddenly had a lot more ground to cover.

Pubic hair: Surprise! The bikini wax originates not in Brazil, but in the Middle East. Many Muslim women remove all the hair from their bodies on the eve of their weddings. Some maintain this fashion throughout their marriages—with their husbands following suit.

Men's beards: Before razors were invented, men reportedly used water and sharp seashells to rip their facial hair out (ouch!); copper razors, developed around 3000 BCE, did the job less painfully. Supposedly, Alexander the Great was one of the first proponents of shaving, believing it helped avoid "dangerous beard-grabbing in combat."

AND THE AWARD FOR LONGEST PUBES GOES TO...

Maoni Vi of Cape Town, whose pubic hair extends twenty-eight inches from her vagina. But wait, there's more (much, much more)—Vi's armpit hair unfurls to thirty-two splendid inches.

PUBIC PENALTY

In Ancient Athens, men who were found guilty of adultery would reportedly be shorn of all their pubic hair.

What do sex and gardening have in common, besides getting dirty?

Both have been found to boost the immune system and relieve depression by increasing serotonin levels in the brain. When you get your hands in the dirt, you come into contact with specific soil bacteria called Mycobacterium vaccae. According to research, these helpful little bacteria trigger the release of serotonin in the brain, inducing anti-depressant effects.

Human, humor, and humility are all derived from humus, the Latin word for earth or dirt. Our ancient relatives were on the same page as the modern-day hippie. These humble, dirt-lovin' humans see horticulture as their birthright. It is inscribed in their DNA to cultivate the earth with care, to grow the freshest GMO-free heirlooms, to nurture organic lacinato kale sprouts with love, and to always give back to the fertile ground that feeds them.

DOUBLE DOPAMINE

Dopamine is a hormone that plays an important role in the reward center of the brain, triggering states of bliss or mild euphoria. One of the main players in the neurochemistry of sex, dopamine is also released— *surprise!*—when we harvest produce from the garden. The dopamine release can be triggered by sight or smell, as well as by the action of actually picking the fruit or vegetable.

GOOD IN BED
THE HIPPIE KAMA SUTRA'S TOP FIVE FOODS TO PLANT IN YOUR GARDEN

ASPARAGUS The original *Kama Sutra* advises to drink it as paste, and rumor has it that some nineteenth century French grooms dined on three meals of asparagus the day before their wedding to ready their libido for the big night.

STRAWBERRIES Legend has it if you break a double strawberry with someone special, it will bring you true love.

ARTICHOKES Dr. Nicolas Venette, a Swedish sexologist, reported that Swedish women who were feeling neglected in the bedroom would serve their husbands artichokes in an effort to increase their desire and stamina.

FIGS In Ancient Greece, where they were believed to be a symbol of love, the arrival of a new fig crop elicited a copulatory ritual.

GARLIC Once upon a time, Tibetan monks were forbidden from entering the monastery if they had been eating garlic because of its reputation for stirring up passions.

BLOOD OF THE EARTH

This delicious blood orange, pomegranate, and beet juice increases mental, physical, and sexual vitality.

INGREDIENTS:
* 6OZ. BLOOD ORANGE JUICE
* 3OZ. BEET JUICE
* 2OZ. POMEGRANATE JUICE
* GINGER (OPTIONAL)

- Peel blood orange and juice.
- Wash beets, cut in small pieces, and juice.
- Peel pomegranate and juice (*or use store-bought pure pomegranate juice*).
- Cut small piece of ginger, leave skin on, and juice.
- Stir.
- Voila!

Ahoy, Matey: Pass the Kraut!

Lacto-fermented foods are such a good source of vitamin C that in the eighteenth century, when the British explorer Captain James Cook sailed, he would bring large barrels of sauerkraut to prevent his crew from getting scurvy on long voyages.

Just Eat it!

Dr. Joseph Mercola and his research team ran a test on fermented vegetables produced by a probiotic starter culture, and found an estimated ten trillion colony-forming units of healthy bacteria. The bottom line? Mercola concluded that a single serving of fermented vegetables could contain more healthful bacteria than an entire bottle of high-potency probiotics.

Rose petals and Barry White may set the mood for some, but a mason jar's worth of homebrewed ginger-mango kombucha is pure hippie Spanish fly. Add a mouthful of caraway-seed sauerkraut, a zesty pinch of kimchi, or a jar of garlicky dill pickles, and you may well provoke orgasm. You are what you eat, and the couple who dines on effervescent fermentations is destined to be cultured, inventive, and highly cosmic.

FERMENTATION: ANCIENT CULTURES

Fermentation is an ancient tradition practiced all around the world. Evidence of winemaking—one of the most popular forms of fermentation—has been found in regions as various as the Caucasus area of Georgia (6000 BCE), Iran (5000 BCE), Ancient Egypt (3150 BCE), pre-Hispanic Mexico (2000 BCE), and Sudan (circa 1500 BCE).

DON'T TOUCH MY FREAKIN' KOMBUCHA!

In 2012, *Gawker* published the increasingly-crazed forwarded emails of a woman working in a New York City nonprofit whose kombucha beverages were repeatedly being stolen from her office's communal fridge. Witness the madness of a woman in love with her kombucha.

Subject: Kombucha Synergy Trilogy (non-alcoholic)—MISSING from 9th floor fridge

Whoever liberated my Synergy Kombucha drink from the 9th floor fridge sometime [t]oday in the past 5 hours—I certainly hope that you plan to replace it. Just because my [sh]arpie wouldn't write on the wet glass bottle doesn't make it fair game.

I hope that you do NOT achieve the re-energizing that you sought. And that the bottle [ex]ploded on you and your clothes as you opened it.

(...) I do not go shopping and transport the potentially explode-y Kombuchas here for you. [Th]ey are for ME to enjoy. A fizzy lift to my afternoon. So, Trilogy is your favorite flavor? Mine, [to]o! You know, maybe you could BRING YOUR OWN. They are not inexpensive items, as you [mu]st know. And this is now number 3 to go missing. WITH MY NAME ON THE BOTTLE.

Whoever you are, I certainly hope that you are overrun with probiotics to the extent [th]at you get thrush-mouth from having binged on my Kombuchas. Also, you ought to know [th]at I have been dubbed the person most likely to kick someone's ass, by a member of senior [ma]nagement who shall remain anonymous. [sic]

"Life is about rhythm. We vibrate, our hearts are pumping blood, we are a rhythm machine. That's what we are."

—Mickey Hart

33

*F*ew events loom more momentous in a hippie's life than a good live show. More than an opportunity to simply dance, groove, laugh, and unify with the collective consciousness, the wacky entrepreneurial mecca found in the parking lot enables amateur chefs and crafty artisans to support and sustain their tour lifestyle. In the mystical world of the shakedown, a hummus burrito is worth its weight in gold, while a yummy grilled cheese, fried in coconut butter and topped with a ripe heirloom tomato, can incite riots of deeply powerful desire.

THE HIPPIE POLL

Why are you going on tour this summer?

- 26%: Backless crocheted halter top accentuates the stomach quite nicely.

- 8%: Met a really hot guy in the parking lot at Deer Creek Phish show in fall '98; must see if he's still there.

- 12%: Pumped to do a little public Hula-Hooping.

- 14%: Nitrous, nitrous, nitrous.

- 39%: Jerry would have wanted it this way.

- 1%: In a monogamous relationship with the Disco Biscuits keyboard player.

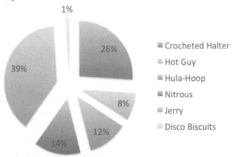

DID YOU KNOW?

The Hacky Sack was invented in 1972 by John Stalberger and Mike Marshall. Beginners work on their stalls, lifts, loops, and clippers, while more adventurous sackers attempt the pendulum, the rainbow, the blur, the jester, mystery meat, the Charlie Brown, the McTwist, and the back stab.

The world's record for consecutive touches on a Hacky Sack is 69,812—accomplished in seven hours, thirty-eight minutes, and twenty-two seconds, on November 15, 1995, by Ted Martin.

Why Aren't You Pursuing the Hacky Sack World Record this year?

- 12%: Demoralizing phobia of Simple brand shoes.

- 18%: Chasing after "world's longest toenails" record instead.

- 29%: No longer welcome in high school parking lots.

- 9%: Seven months pregnant; fear for safety of unborn child when performing the "Flying Clipper."

- 16%: Holding out for Cliff Bar sponsorship offer.

- 12%: Better suited to dog-eat-dog world of Frisbee Golf.

- 4%: Just not that good at kicking things.

*T*his versatile, non-psychotropic variety of *Cannabis sativa* is the ultimate shapeshifter, gracefully transforming into hemp paper, hemp wax, hemp resin, hemp cloth, hemp oil, hemp fuel, or hemp flour, according to need. Hemp car doors and hemp sink basins are now bio-plastic realities; hemp waffles, hemp tofu, and hemp nut butters make a yummy, healthy snack. Sustainably sexy, economical, and durable, the hippie's love affair with this magical plant is truly built to last.

HOMEMADE HEMP MILK

Hemp milk is not only delicious, it's rich in ten essential amino acids, meaning it's a useful source of vegan protein. More digestible than soy milk, It's also incredibly easy to make—and unlike almond milk, you don't have to soak the seeds overnight. Try it!

INGREDIENTS

1 CUP HEMP SEEDS

3 TO 4 CUPS WATER (3 CUPS FOR THICKER MILK, 4 CUPS FOR THINNER)

1 TBSP. OF COCONUT OIL

2 TBSP. OF RAW HONEY OR A FEW DROPS OF STEVIA

1/2 TBSP. OF ORGANIC VANILLA POWDER

A PINCH OF HIMALAYAN PINK SALT (OR OTHER UNPROCESSED SEA SALT)

DIRECTIONS

In a high speed blender, add hemp and water. Blend on high for about two minutes, or until fully liquified. Strain into a wide glass bowl through a milk bag (you can find milk bags online or at a health food store). Discard the hemp fibers from the bag. Rinse the blender and pour the milk back into the blender from the bowl. Add coconut oil, honey or stevia, vanilla powder, and salt. Blend briefly.

42

Hempstory

- Henry Ford's first Model-T was built to run on hemp gasoline. The car itself was constructed from hemp and wheat straw. The Model-T boasted hemp plastic panels whose impact strength was many times greater than steel. Ford, who kept hemp fields on his large estate, advertised the car as having been "grown from the soil."

- Both George Washington and Thomas Jefferson grew hemp on their Virginia farms. In fact, hemp was such a successful cash crop that in the 1760s, it was legal in some Virginia counties to pay taxes in hemp.

- Japan has a religious tradition which requires that the Emperor wear hemp garments. A small plot of hemp is maintained strictly for the imperial family.

- The original Levi Strauss jeans were made from hemp. So was the original version of the Declaration of Independence.

Want to Be a Hemp Farmer?

Well, it's still complicated. If you live in North Dakota, Hawaii, Kentucky, Maine, Maryland, Oregon, California, Montana, West Virginia, or Vermont, you might be in luck. As of 2014, hemp cultivation is technically legal there, though farmers have yet to really begin growing due to DEA (Drug Enforcement Agency) resistance.

However, after marijuana was legalized for recreational purposes in Colorado, a few farmers planted and harvested several acres of hemp, bringing in the first official legal hemp crop in the United States in over fifty years.

nusually sensitive to life-energy, and uncommonly enthusiastic about wearing comfortable pants, hippies have been ahead of the yoga curve for quite some time now, performing gymnastic feats of sacramental union like it ain't no thing. Flexible, strong, and sexy, they push forward on rubber mats, intertwining limbs, standing upon their hands, envisioning karmic resolution, inner peace, and spiritual gratification.

APHRODISIAFACT:

In one study published in the 2007 *Journal of Sexual Medicine*, sixty-eight Indian men living in New Dehli who suffered from premature ejaculation were made to undergo a three-month course of yoga, practicing poses like Paschimottanasana (seated forward bend), Halasana (plow), Sarvangasana (shoulder-stand), Matsyasana (fish), and Dhanurasana (bow) on a daily basis. One hundred percent of the men showed statistically significant improvement and reported increased sexual satisfaction.

The Hippie Poll

The guy practicing on the mat next to you is quite cute. What are you doing to attract him?

- 5%: Seductively chanting Om, in multiorgasmic, Earth goddess way.
- 29%: Wishing you'd worn the good yoga pants today, dammit.
- 13%: Cutting way back on the downward-dog farting.
- 20%: Slowly drenching self in sweat, panting like a horse.
- 32%: Planning post-Shavasana invite to all-tempeh buffet.
- 1%: Readying to talk dirty in Hindi, if necessary.

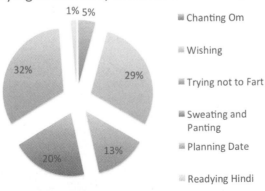

"The more we sweat in peace, the
less we bleed in war."
                —Vijaya Lakshmi Pandit

THE HOT AND SWEATY FACTS

- An average person sweats around one liter per hour while exercising.

- Women have more sweat glands than men, but men produce more sweat.

- Every day, about five million gallons of sweat are produced by people having sex around the world.

- During sweaty sex, men emanate testosterone. Perspiration can be a biological turn-on for women.

- Habitual exposure during intercourse to the hormones contained in male armpit sweat reportedly leads to more regular menstrual cycles.

- Having sex while sick often reduces a fever, due to the sweat produced.

- Sweat glands are the most concentrated on the bottom of our feet.

- Lips don't have sweat glands. Because sweat glands tend to keep skin moisturized, lips tend to dry out faster than the rest of the body.

You Know it's Someone's First Time in a Sweat Lodge When They...

- Ask for the Wi-Fi password.
- Crack open a refreshing Coors Light.
- Send a "shout out to all my ancestors, and one to Biggie."
- Snap a selfie with the lodge elder upon entering ceremony.
- Request for group singalong of "Free Bird."

BLESS YOU:
HOW TO SMUDGE, IN SIX EASY STEPS

What You'll Need:

ABALONE SHELL OR SMUDGE BOWL
APPROPRIATE HERBS
SOURCE OF FIRE (LIGHTER OR MATCHES)
FEATHER

Begin by looking into the eyes of your partner. Fan the smoke to their heart. Move up the right side of the body, around the head, moving clockwise, peacefully cleansing them with the smoke. Continue down left side, smudging their shoulder, arm, torso, leg, and foot. Maintaining a clockwise motion, move up the right side of the body. Turn your partner around and repeat these movements as you smudge and bless their back.

A Beginner's Guide to Smudging

You know you really need to smudge when . . .

- On your romantic getaway weekend, you pitch your Coleman tent, aka "The Love Den," on an Indian burial ground.

- You're at Ecstatic Dance and the sweat from everyone's prayers is so thick and stinky you could cut it with a knife.

- You get dry-humped by a Labrador during an ayahuasca ceremony.

- You're on public transportation and a methamphetamine-fueled troll sits on your lap, plants a big wet one on you, and murmurs, "I love you, man."

- Your best friend confesses that you "give him a boner sometimes."

SACRED HERBS: HEALING POWERS

SAGE: When a person enters ceremony or a sacred space, sage is used to bless, heal, and rid the person of unwanted influences.

CEDAR: Medicine of protection, cedar is used to purify a new home, inviting unwanted spirits to depart peacefully.

SWEETGRASS: Also called seneca grass, vanilla grass, and holy grass, sweetgrass is the essence of the feminine, reminding us of mother Earth's abundance.

LAVENDER: Calming and cleansing, lavender is used for inviting spirits.

COPAL: This tree sap, or "blood of the trees," is good for psychic work. Native peoples often use copal as an offering to the gods.

FRANKINCENSE: This interdenominationally-beloved tree resin eases depression, promotes clairvoyance, and protects the soul.

MYRRH: Maintains a state of enlightenment. It connects to the spirit of youth and clears the path to one's own truth.

omewhere over the rainbow in Northern California, where the hills are south-facing and the land is green, lies Trim Camp, the heart of the cannabis industry. The sound of snipping scissors and the aphrodisiac aroma of skunky buds fill the air. Day in and day out, trimmers with trichome-encrusted fingers tediously prepare the THC-laden medicine for consumption. "Get that ganja, bubonic chronic, sticky-icky, pakalolo, cigga-weed" rings through their minds. And in a whirlwind of flying buds, stems, seeds, and hash, a cannabliss frenzy of sticky crystal-covered humans ensues.

DID YOU KNOW?

The first documented use of medicinal marijuana is by Chinese emperor Shen Nung, in 2737 BCE. The emperor believed that cannabis cured pains associated with rheumatism and gout.

"Yesterday, Colorado Governor John Hickenlooper signed an amendment that officially legalized marijuana in the state. Stoners took a moment to thank Governor Hickenlooper, then they spent a few hours just saying the word 'Hickenlooper.'"

—Jimmy Fallon

I'LL HAVE A TRIPLE NON-FAT ONE-GRAM INDICA SPLIFF, PLEASE...

In 2013, there were more registered medical marijuana dispensaries in Los Angeles than Starbucks franchises.

HOMEMADE COCONUT-OIL CANNABIS LUBE

Holed up at a trim camp in Humboldt, and you've just run out of Astroglide? Have no fear! Cannabis-infused coconut oil will do the trick nicely, moisturizing and stimulating but not intoxicating you. (Unless you start to eat it!)

INGREDIENTS:
2 OZ. TRIM OR FRESH PRUNINGS
1 CUP ORGANIC COCONUT OIL

DIRECTIONS: Using a Crock-Pot, gently melt your coconut oil over low heat. Add trim, stirring every fifteen minutes to infuse your mixture with cannabinoids.

After a few hours of steeping, turn the heat off and allow the oil to cool. Using a large spoon or ladle, scoop the mixture into a clean French press. Press. The goal is to separate the plant matter from your cannabis oil. You may have to do this a few times.

Pour the clean oil into bowl or jar. Cover and refrigerate. Enjoy!

"Take down a musical instrument. Let the beauty we love be what we do. There are hundreds of ways to kneel and kiss the ground."

—Rumi

Somewhere, in a far-off corner of a national forest in Oregon, a strange group of mystical faeries, wild-eyed warlocks, and enchanting wood nymphs gather. They are the Rainbow Family: a loosely-strung collective of hard-core mushroom-chomping anticapitalist pagans who love nothing more than downing a few bowls of vegan stew and partying hard in Mother Nature's kitchen. In the free-spirited realm of the Rainbow, love is always in the air: a full-spectrum fantasy of psychedelic soul communion, freak-flag-flying mischief, and purely bohemian rapture.

AN YOU SPEAK RAINBOW?

A short glossary of helpful terms to get you through your first Gathering

A-Camp: Alcohol Camp, a place where chronic alcohol drinkers congregate and drink, usually on the perimeter of a Gathering.

Babylon: The world outside of the Gathering.

Bliss Ninny: An overly-spiritual attendee, out of touch with the physical realities and demands of the environment.

Faerie: Gay male Rainbow.

Ground Score: Item of value that is found on the ground.

Heartsong: Personal feelings, emotions, observations, and visions as articulated at Gatherings.

Hug Patrol: A group who wander around the Gathering, hugging people.

Shanti Sena: The peacekeeping counsel. Difficult problems are commonly referred to the Shanti Sena.

Shitter: A Rainbow latrine. Dig one, it's a religious experience.

Sisters' Space: An area reserved exclusively for women.

Six-Up: Armed police officer.

Wahwah: A tasty morsel of food, easy to eat, but not a meal. (*from prison slang*)

We Love You: Common greeting, usually shouted in unison by a group of people.

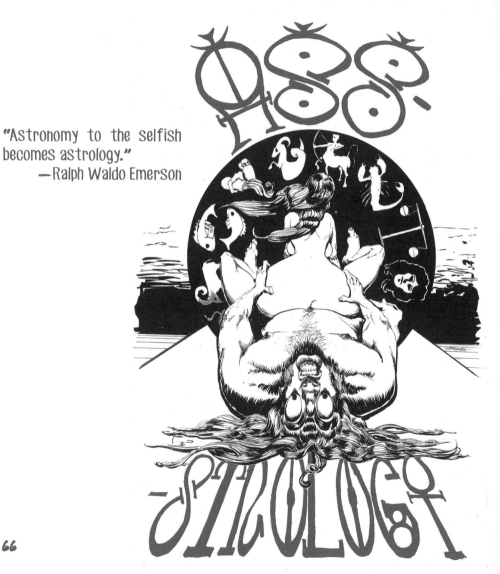

"Astronomy to the selfish becomes astrology."
—Ralph Waldo Emerson

As esteemed as atomic science, as revered as the holy *Bible*, astrology is a beacon of truth and divination for the sensitive, moon-worshipping souls known as hippies—particularly in the realm of love and relationships. It is of utter importance to these starry-eyed souls which heavenly bodies are influencing their lovers, as the compatibility of rising signs and conjunctions of the cosmos could make or break their chemistry in the sack. With natal charts bedside and the zodiac as their guide, they plunge in, always on the hunt for a juicy full moon.

HOUSE OF STARS

Ronald Reagan, fortieth President of the United States and notorious hippie-hater, was a true believer in the power of the stars. After an assassination attempt nearly took Reagan's life in 1981, he and his wife Nancy consistently sought the advice of a San Francisco astrologer Joan Quigley, building a strong and influential relationship. When White House Chief of Staff Donald Regan left the cabinet in 1987, he wrote, "virtually every major move and decision the Reagans made during my time as White House Chief of Staff was cleared in advance with a woman in San Francisco [Quiqley] who drew up horoscopes to make certain that the planets were in a favorable alignment for the enterprise."

BORN UNDER A BAD SIGN

Winona Dimeo-Ediger & Katelyn Kollinzas, resident astrology experts at *The Frisky*, explore the most likely addictions for each astrological sign.

ARIES: Ritalin. It's the Aries way to try to speed up life as much as humanly possible, even it means popping pills to amp up the intensity.

TAURUS: Food. It is all too easy to take your natural love of food to an addictive level.

GEMINI: Cigarettes. What starts as a way for you to channel your nervous energy in social settings can easily become a nasty pack-a-day addiction.

CANCER: Painkillers. Your constant heightened state of emotional intensity can leave you reaching for pills as a way to numb the pain.

LEO: Gambling. You love the thrill of big risks, the high of winning, and the cheering crowds.

VIRGO: Valium. Your high-strung, perfectionist ways often turn you into a bundle of nerves. When you want to chill out, Valium can seem like a quick fix.

LIBRA: Alcohol. What may start out as a social habit to relax you at parties can transform into an addiction you indulge every night, whether you're out at the bar or home alone.

SCORPIO: Sex. Your passionate and obsessive personality paired with an extremely high sex drive makes you the perfect candidate for a full-blown sex addiction.

SAGITTARIUS: Exercise. Combine your body perfectionism with your need for physical activity and you could easily develop an unhealthy obsession with your treadmill.

CAPRICORN: Shopping. As much as you love making money, you also love accumulating fancy things, which can lead to an overabundance of expensive possessions.

AQUARIUS: Drug experimentation. As an open-minded person, you'll try anything once.

PISCES: Marijuana. Your love of leisure and go-with-the-flow attitude makes pot your obvious drug of choice.

"Most Freegans are both resourceful and adventurous. They have an ability to adapt and find the good in situations that are otherwise just a dump."

Interview with a Freegan

Writer Amanda Green interviewed a couple of young Freegans about romance, relationship, and dumpster love.

Does a potential romantic partner of yours have to be a freegan?

No, but they have to be down with anticapitalism and eating food from the trash.

What's the best reason to date a freegan?

Most freegans are both resourceful and adventurous. They have an ability to adapt and find the good in situations that are otherwise just a dump.

What's your idea of the perfect freegan date?

The perfect freegan date would be a combination of scavenging and then enjoying the spoils of the scavenge. Ideally, we'd have a bike with a bike trailer or a tandem bike to take dumpstering. When we'd get to the dumpster, it would be full of smoothies and vegan sausage and pasta. That would get us hot. After some hot making out on a pile of tortilla chips in the dumpster, we'd have hot, sweaty, nasty sex.

Free Movements

The Really, Really Free Market (RRFM)

A horizontally-organized collective whose stated aim is to counteract capitalism through resource sharing and activism, these markets usually take place in open community spaces and offer both goods and services. RRFM's exist in Fairbanks, Salt Lake City, Colorado Springs, Carrboro, Buffalo, Chicago, Baltimore, Grand Rapids, Providence, Austin, Olympia, Moscow, London, Chennai, and many other locales!

The Freecycle Network

A grassroots and nonprofit movement who lives by the mantra reduce, reuse, recycle—and avoid the landfill. With over seven million members around the world, freecycling is steadily growing in popularity.

The Free Box

One person's trash is another person's treasure. Pillars of magic and portals of manifestation in intentional communities around the world, Free boxes are the optimal place from which to shed layers, and then acquire exciting, one-of-a-kind outfits. Where else can you donate a pair of snakeskin boots and unearth the alpaca sweater of your dreams?

"The '60s are gone. Dope will never be as cheap, sex never as free, and the rock and roll never as great."

—Abbie Hoffman

74

*H*ippies are like fine wine: They ripen with age. Even if they're no longer soaring on Sandoz acid at a Dead show, like in the good ol' days, or riding a freedom bus through Mississippi, hearts rising in their chests, career hippies are generally still game to catch some good jazz in the city or fondle organic zucchini at a local farmers market. On anniversaries, they soak in sulfur baths; at family reunions, they sneak around back for a quick pre-game toke. And while their pulses may have slowed, aging flower children still love to make love. If you listen, late at night you can hear them knockin' Birkenstocks.

SEX SYMBOLS OF THE BIRKENSTOCK

Celebrating the magical women of the 1960s counterculture

JONI MITCHELL: Canadian. Devil-may-care. Inventive, soulful. Talented painter, heavy smoker. Jazz explorer. Romantically linked to Peter Coyote, James Taylor, Jack Nicholson, and Leonard Cohen.

JOAN BAEZ: Powerful, intelligent, the voice of peace and freedom. One-time lover of Bob Dylan.

JANIS JOPLIN: Boozy, humble, rebellious. Talented, earthy. Born in Port Arthur, Texas. Early ally of R. Crumb; madly in love with the Grateful Dead's Ron "Pigpen" McKernan. Dead at twenty-seven.

JANE FONDA: Rich girl turned *Playboy* pin-up/sci-fi spoof sex star. Prominent anti-Vietnam protestor; falsely arrested for drug smuggling in 1970. Aerobics innovator. Wife of CNN billionaire Ted Turner.

GRACE SLICK: LSD-tinged. Powerful pipes. Fave of Hunter S. Thompson. Daughter China Wing, born 1971, reportedly intended to have been named "God." Oldest female vocalist, at forty-six, to score #1 Billboard Hit ("We Built This City," 1985, Jefferson Starship).

STEVIE NICKS: "The Best Hippie Queen Earth Mother" (said *Rolling Stone*). Leathery, magical. Shawls, lace, cocaine, and platforms. Rumored strong interest in Wicca and witchcraft. Present-day hipster girls in LA spend a lot of money trying to dress exactly like her.

GLORIA STEINEM: Original feminist. Born in Toledo, Ohio. Bespectacled, sexy. Half-Jewish, Phi Beta Kappa. Worked as *Playboy* Bunny at New York Playboy Club for three months in 1963. Founder of *Ms. Magazine* in 1972. Quotable: "If men could get pregnant, abortion would be a sacrament."

Great Moments from the Heart of an Era

1967

- The world's first ATM is utilized at Barclays Bank in England.

- *Rolling Stone*'s first issue comes off the presses.

- National Organization for Women (NOW) holds its first national conference.

- Human Be-In takes place in San Francisco's Golden Gate Park, setting the stage for the Summer of Love.

- Thurgood Marshall becomes the first African American Justice of United States Supreme Court.

- Clinton Corn Processing Co. pioneers high-fructose corn syrup.

- Thousands protest the Vietnam War during a march on Washington. Allen Ginsberg chants to levitate the Pentagon.

1968

- Price of a first-class stamp increases to six cents.

- First Jacuzzi is introduced at California's Orange County Fair.

- Virginia Slims, first cigarette marketed to women, is popularized—"Slims" is a reminder that smoking is not fattening.

- Yale University opens its doors to women.

- Hot Wheels toy cars are introduced by Mattel.

- The musical *Hair* opens on Broadway.

- Tom Wolfe publishes *The Electric Kool-Aid Acid Test*, the definitive insider's take on hippie adventurers Ken Kesey and the Merry Pranksters.

- Johnny Cash plays Folsom Prison.

- Andy Warhol survives an assassination attempt.

1969

- *Midnight Cowboy* becomes the first and only X-rated film to win the Best Picture Oscar.

- Stonewall riots in New York City mark the beginning of the modern-day gay rights movement.

- The GAP—named for the "generation gap"—opens its first store in San Francisco, selling records and blue jeans.

- First-ever episode of *Scooby-Doo* is broadcast on CBS.

- John Lennon and Yoko Ono spend their honeymoon staging a Bed-In for peace in Amsterdam.

- Children's Television Workshop introduces the first episode of *Sesame Street*.

- More than 500,000 gather in upstate New York to celebrate four days of peace, love, and music at Woodstock.

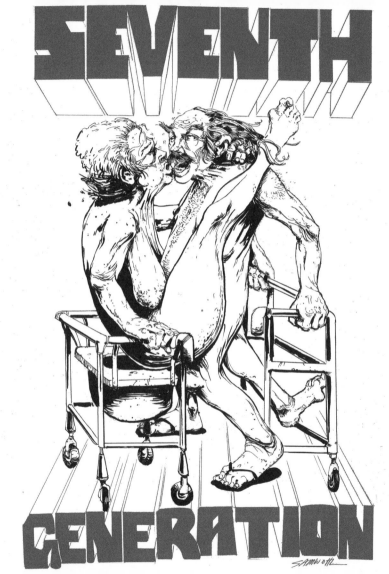

SEVENTH

GENERATION

The Great Law of the Iroquois guides our elders to make decisions today that will benefit the children seven generations into the future. Whether these silver-haired sages are channeling their passion into creating an ecological, sustainable future for the youth, or ushering their partner into a mind-altering state of orgasmic bliss, they know full well the power their reverberations and gyrations have on the world.

WHO'S YOUR DADDY?

Indian farmer Nanu Ram Jogi is thought to be the world's oldest father. The ninety-year-old, now married to his fourth wife, says he's not exactly sure how many children he's produced, but reports that he has "at least" twenty-one children. Jogi plans to keep up the babymaking until he passes the century mark.

IN YO' FACE!

Recently, when Heather Locklear was asked if she had any suggestions for anti-aging products, she answered, "You just put semen on your face." As it turns out, she was on to something: Spermine, one of the components of semen, is high in powerful anti-oxidantants, and can be used to decrease wrinkles, moisturize and smooth the skin, even heal sunburn.

Apparently, the trend is catching on: In recent years, Bioforskning, a Norwegian beauty company, synthesized spermine into a moisturizing facial cream, while another company, Cmen Beauty Now, discreetly delivered fresh semen to homes, all in the name of healthy skin. And, believe it or not, spermine facials are available at several high-end spas.

BETTER LIVING THROUGH ORGASM

- The *Journal of the American Medical Association* states that "high ejaculation frequency was related to decreased risk of total prostate cancer."

- The hormone DHEA is released in response to sexual excitement and orgasm. DHEA strengthens immunity, improves mental functioning, and relieves depression.

- Good sex really does make you glow. Women who have regular sex have higher levels of estrogen and produce more collagen, which is essential to maintaining healthier, smoother skin. Healthy levels of estrogen also help to protect us from heart disease, osteoporosis, and Alzheimer's.

The laws of attraction are inherently animalistic, governed by powerful chains of pheromones and irresistible natural odors. From musky to skunky, spicy to sweet, the unadulterated hippie armpit is notoriously aromatic, aphrodisiacal, and erogenous. High on the intelligence of olfaction, passionate neo-primitives plunge their sniffers into these fragrant caverns, sniffing and licking their way to raw, sensual bliss.

SMELLS FROM AROUND THE WORLD

- Among the Desana tribe of the Amazon, marriage can only occur between people of different odors. The Batek Negrito tribe of the Malay Peninsula agrees: Not only can you not marry or make love to someone with your odor, sitting too close to them for long is considered treacherous.

- For the Serer Ndut of Senegal, body odor transcends death: The Ndut believe they can know precisely which ancestor has been reincarnated in the next generation by comparing the likeness of a child's scent to that of the deceased.

- To the Dogon of Mali, the scent of an onion is highly intoxicating. Men rub fried onions over their bodies, creating a powerful perfume.

- Among the cattle-centric culture of the Dassanetch of Ethiopia, the scent of cows is extremely desirable. Men wash their hands in cattle urine, or bedaub their bodies with manure in order to attract potential mates.

DID YOU KNOW?

The human nose can remember up to 50,000 different scents.

NATURAL MYSTIC: HOW TO MAKE YOUR OWN AMAZING, ALL-NATURAL HIPPIE-APPROVED DEODORANT

This recipe is astoundingly simple, and incredibly effective. You'll never smell like a hippie again (unless, of course, you want to).

INGREDIENTS:

1/4 CUP BAKING SODA
1/4 CUP CORNSTARCH
4-6 TBSP. COCONUT OIL
(Depending on how stiff you want the product to be)
TEA TREE OIL, 5-20 DROPS (OPTIONAL)

Place ingredients in glass bowl and mix together. Scoop the resulting paste into a plastic container, or hollow out an old deodorant and use the canister to contain your new beauty product. Place in fridge to firm. To use, rub a small amount underarm.

Viagra? Cialis? Phssst. Hippie guys don't care for the blue pills. Instead, they're much more likely to check out natural playtime alternatives, like yohimbe, a virility-inducing herbal supplement derived from the bark of an African tree, or Epimedium, an herbaceous Chinese perennial also known as horny goat weed. From gingko to maca, Mother Nature's plant allies have been trusted aphrodisiacs for centuries, granting enlightened couples an extra stiff boost in their friskiest times of need.

> "God gave man a penis and a brain, but not enough blood to use both at the same time."
> —Robin Williams

TOP 7 MOVIES THAT SOUND LIKE THEY COULD ALSO BE ABOUT PENISES

SHAFT
FREE WILLY
THE NUTTY PROFESSOR
THE COLOR PURPLE
THE HARDER THEY COME
FAST & FURIOUS
HOOK

The Naked Truth: Secrets of the Penis

By restricting flow to blood vessels, smoking can shorten penises by up to a centimeter.

A *Men's Health* survey reports that 71% of men have "growers," while 29% have "show-ers."

Reportedly, one man in every 400 is flexible enough to give himself oral pleasure.

Fetuses can achieve erections. Male babies are often born in a state of arousal.

A study at the University of Oslo in Norway shows that primates with bigger testicles are more likely to be unfaithful in sexual relationships.

A typical ejaculation—about 3.4 milliliters—contains less than one calorie.

The word avocado is derived from the Aztec word *ahuacati*, meaning testicle.

Males don't need a functioning brain to ejaculate—that command originates from the spinal cord.

One in every five or six million males is born with a condition called diphallus, also known as having two penises.

Koro, or "penis panic," is a condition of mass hysteria wherein groups of men believe their penises are in jeopardy of disappearing.

The average speed of ejaculation is twenty-eight miles per hour.

Pigs have curly penises and straight tails.

Dolphins have muscular, S-shaped penises that they use to grab objects. They are frequent masturbators, adding to their reputation as joyful mammals.

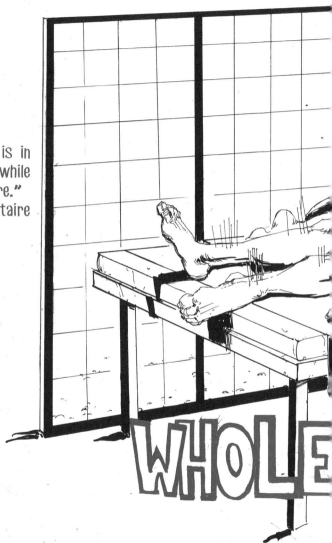

"The art of medicine is in amusing a patient while nature affects the cure."
                                                    —Voltaire

IN - ONE

Hippies are complex creatures, true believers in the mysterious entanglement of mind, body, and spirit. Many perceive the invisible energy known as chi pulsing through them, and whether by means of a needle in the third eye, a subtle adjustment to the cerebral-sacral fluid, or a double-terminated Tantric Twin Rose Quartz laid on the heart chakra, when the channels open, the energy flows—sometimes to all the right places.

ACUPUNCTURE AND FERTILITY:

One study by German researchers found that including acupuncture with the traditional IVF treatment protocols substantially increased pregnancy success. One hundred and sixty women were involved in the study; one group of eighty women received twenty-five minute acupuncture treatments before and directly after having a fertilized embryo transferred into their uterus, while the other group of women did not receive acupuncture.

Both groups had pregnancies, but the acupuncture group had thirty-four, compared to twenty-one for the women who received IVF alone.

THE HOLISTIC CHALLENGE:

Acupuncture too humdrum for you? Try one of these unique natural therapies:

Urotherapy: The drinking of one's own urine and massaging one's skin with one's own urine. Morarji Desai, an Indian prime minisiter, once stated that urine therapy was the perfect medical solution for Indians who could not afford medical treatment.

Kambo: An injection of Amazonian tree frog venom by way of bamboo sticks. There are a wide range of medical applications, including Alzheimer's, migraines, inflammation, infection, cancer, and fertility problems in women and men.

Hot Sand Therapy: Being buried in the sand during the hottest time of the day. Said to treat rheumatism, joint pain, and sexual impotency.

Apitherapy: Bee acupuncture therapy and bee venom can help treat illnesses such as arthritis, cancer, and multiple sclerosis.

JUST THE TIPS:

To awaken sexual energy and increase pleasure during lovemaking, hold, press, or suck related acupressure points. Be creative!

Bubbling Springs: Sole of the foot, at base of the ball between the two pads.

Sea of Vitality: On the lower back, between the second and third lumbar vertebrae, two to three finger widths from spine.

Sea of Energy: Three finger widths directly below belly button.

Rushing Door: Pelvic area, in the middle of the crease where leg joins the trunk.

GS

"Our bodies were printed as blank pages
to be filled with the ink of our hearts."
—Michael Biondi

Deep in the heart of urban America, an unconventional neohippie tribe lurks: the modern primitive. Aesthetically bold, sweetly masochistic, these devotees of body art value self-expression and individuality above all else. Adrenaline enthusiasts, experts in the neurochemistry of pain, you'll often find them in pairs; skins drenched in designs, lobes gaping and gauged, these lovers live large, always wearing their art on their sleeve.

THE ILLUSTRATED MAN

Performance artist Gregory Paul McLaren, also known as Lucky Diamond Rich, is the most tattooed living human, sporting designs on every square inch of his body, including the inside of his foreskin, mouth, and ears.

The Hole Truth

- One of the earliest known people to sport stretched ear lobes was ancient Egyptian pharaoh King Tutankhamen. It's unclear as to what instrument was used to stretch the pharaoh's ears, though possibilities include bamboo or wooden plugs.

- Lip piercing and lip stretching have their roots in African and South American tribal cultures; in regions of Malawi, women adorned their lips with a lip disc called a pelele that could eventually reach several inches of diameter.

- Tongue piercing was practiced by the Aztec and Mayan cultures; nobility were said to pierce their tongues with thorns, then collect the blood on pieces of bark, burning them as an act of reverence to their gods.

- Nipple piercing was said to have been a sign of masculinity for soldiers of Ancient Rome.

- Shakespeare, Sir Walter Raleigh, and Charles I all wore one earring in Elizabethan-era England. In the European Middle Ages, sailors tended to pierce their ears for insurance purposes: if they died at sea, the earring could be used to pay for their burial.

- Many Native American and Alaskan tribes practiced septum piercing. Males in New Guinea traditionally adorned their pierced septums with bones and feathers, status symbols that spoke of the wearer's wealth and virility.

"Freedom is just chaos, with better lighting."
—Alan Dean Foster

A wild desert celebration of synchronicity, radical self-expression, psychedelic adventuring, and all-night dance parties, Burning Man is an avant-garde hippie paradise. Refreshingly bizarre, magically unique, the postmodern wonderland known as Black Rock City vibrates and shimmers with a fantastical fusion of creative and sexual energy. Every inch teems with sculpture, sounds, performance, and wonder—though the most resplendent works of art you'll see at Burning Man are likely its jaw-droppingly sexy citizens. Costume-clad, covered in dust, these courageous, open-hearted freaks cuddle tight, grasping lovers new and old, in love with the universe, tasting the nectar of life.

Top 13 Reasons Why You Didn't Have Sex at Burning Man

- Ate too many mushrooms; was convinced my partner was an evil troll.
- Hurt my testicles trying to mount a double-decker bike.
- The pee jug in the tent elicited waves of revulsion.
- Two words: playa pussy.
- No money exchange at BRC; I'm used to paying for it.
- Bartered the majority of my condoms for a faux-fur top hat and crushed velvet cape.
- Does getting fingered on a dance floor count?
- Was satisfied getting penetrated by bass.
- Wasn't in a partner agreement contract before I went.
- The approximately three pounds of dust I inhaled fucked with my libido.
- Tried; I suffered heatstroke in the tent.
- It conflicted with my sworn duties as an undercover federal agent.
- Shirtcocked my way to celibacy, yet again.

"When you're making love under LSD, it's as though every cell in your body is making love with every cell in her body. Your hand doesn't caress her skin but sinks down into and merges with ancient dynamos of ecstasy within her."
—Timothy Leary

Down the rabbit hole and into the wacky world of psychedelia, you will find the most adventurous of hippies, slipping and sliding through interdimensional travel and shape shifting between archetypal characters. A fistful of psilocybin, a few tablets of white lightning, or a toke of the spirit molecule will tinker with the neurotransmitters, inducing unexpected, mind-bending states of consciousness. It is here, beyond the veil with third eye opened, in the reflection of the beloved, that only one truth remains: we are one.

TALES FROM BEYOND:

Here's what hippies had to say about their experience of sex on psychedelics

"LSD and sex? I can't tell when it began, or when it ended." —Skywalker

"It was a rebirthing into dolphin consciousness." —Akasha Divinity

"It's a whole lotta hype, couldn't get my parts working, it was one big snugglefest." —Chris Alis

"You know how everyone is always saying we are one and shit? Well, I felt that. It's for real, yo!" —Artsy Phartsy

"You usually need to communicate to get to that point, I have never gotten that far." —Brock Lee

"We had sex, but it wasn't like the sex you are thinking. It was eye sex, fingers intertwining sex, sun sex, voice sex, you touch my soul sex. The best kind." —Pooja Love

"I made love to the Earth. I know it sounds weird, but yes I actually had intercourse with the ground." —Jon Doe

earth first

"I have to tell you the coolest people I've ever met, young and old, are the ones who are out there giving their life for a good cause. They glow more; they're the most beautiful, magnificent, powerful people I've ever seen. They're much more powerful than the richest person and more beautiful than any model, because their beauty and power resonates from deep within the life force all the way through their body, and shines out."

—Julia "Butterfly" Hill

Cradled in the ancient arms of the Redwoods, bare skin pressed firmly against wet mossy bark, passionate Earth stewards stop at nothing to protect Mama Nature's forests. Come lockdown or tree-sit, these dendrophilious hippies rise up in solidarity with the wild. Brave and devoted, endearingly radical, nature lovers such as these always seem to be barking up the right tree.

NATURAL ATTRACTION

Twenty-one-year old Scottish man William Shaw has been banned for life from Central Park in Airdrie, Scotland for crimes relating to hardwood. Reportedly, Shaw tried to have sex with a "tree while his trousers were around his ankles." Shaw pleaded not guilty, and was released on the condition he stay far from the park.

Said one of Shaw's neighbors: "I have seen him about, and he seems a quiet lad."

THE ACORN DOESN'T FALL FAR FROM THE TREE

In 2013, a Peruivan environmental activist and actor named Richard Torres married a tree, whom he named "Aliehuen Neuhen," in an official ceremony in Buenos Aires, Argentina.

"**P**eople are making love in such a hurry," chuckles spiritual leader Osho, "as if they want to finish it as quickly as possible." Not so for devotees of tantra, who accord to the divine law of slow is sexy. Mystically-minded, transcendental, and calm, these dedicated lovers deftly align their chakras, slipping into states of heightened erotic awareness and rising kundalini. With synchonized breath, and soft gazes, sex might not get much more magical than this.

NOT-SO-TANTRIC PICK-UP LINES

♪ "I don't want to make love to you just yet; I just want to dance with your energy."

♪ "When I first laid eyes on you, my second chakra started twerking."

♪ "Wanna come over to my crystal yoni cave, for a private tantra puja?"

♪ "Do you mind if I chant dirty to you?"

♪ "Why don't you astral-travel into my bedroom?"

♪ "I came into a heightened state of awareness after I saw that ass."

5 WAYS TO CONNECT BEFORE YOU CONNECT

May your lovemaking be infused with trust and connectedness.

- Design an Intimacy Space: Clear your special love zone of any clutter. Burn sage, palo santo, or other sacred herbs. Add fresh flowers, or create an altar. Devise a sense of openness that you may fill with your shared pleasure.

- Partner stretching: Ideally, the entire body is active and receptive as you make love, ushering the experience out of the head and into the whole being. Take some time to stretch together before venturing into intimacy. Use your partner's strength and flexibility to mobilize your every limb.

- Eye gazing: Be brave! It's hard to hide when you're looking deep into your partner's eyes, but the awkwardness or vulnerability you may feel in the moment will likely give way to tenderness and a deeper sense of connectedness—and that can carry over in exciting ways when you begin to join physically.

- Breathe each other's breath: Synchronize with one another. Imagine for a moment you are inside your lover's body. Let their heartbeat be your own. Breathe and relax.

- Nonsexual touch: Explore your lover's body with curious fingers, not for the purpose of seduction, but for the pure pleasure of touch. Be open to any sensation. Be open to surprise. Play for as long as you like.

THE SINGULARITY

"Don't knock masturbation.
It's sex with someone I love."
—Woody Allen

LET THE RIVERS RISE

In Ancient Egypt, the current of the Nile River was thought to be controlled by creation God Atum's ejaculation. Egyptian pharaohs, believing themselves earthly representatives of the god, ritually masturbated into the Nile, in order to ensure an abundance of water.

FLAKES FOR PURITY

Kellogg's Corn Flakes were originally invented as part of antimasturbation campaign by super-stodgy Michigan physician John Harvey Kellogg. The doctor, believing sex was ruinous to physical and spiritual well-being, never consummated his marriage; he and his wife slept in separate rooms and adopted children. The blandness of Corn Flakes were just one idea he had to curb self-love. He also supported bandaging teenagers' hands, covering their genitals with patented cages, and, when necessary, using electric shock therapy.

MASTURBATE-A-THON

In 2009, Masanobu Sato of Japan masturbated for nine hours and fifty-eight minutes at the Center for Sex and Culture in San Francisco, earning himself the title of world record holder masturbator.

Innovative, Environmentally-Friendly, Hippie-Babe-Approved Tools for Self-Love

- Babeland's Solar-Bullet Vibe: Eight hours of sun provides one hour of blissful two-speed vibration. Bring it to Burning Man or your next camping trip to Yosemite.

- Laid Stone Dildo: This sex toy, made of polished Norwegian Moonstone, is not only beautiful and luxurious, it's recycled, constructed by reusing the small stone pieces that would normally be discarded by a quarry.

- Nob Essence All-Natural Organic Hardwood Dildo: This woman-owned company produces hardwood "sex sculptures"—gorgeously crafted, made from renewable raw materials. And yes, they promise, you won't get splinters.

- Organic Cucumber: Doesn't get much more Earth-friendly than this. Directions: Head to farmer's market. Select cool, appealing, locally-grown cuke. Try not to giggle as you pay.

AUTHOR PHOTO BY MICHELLE MAGDALENA

SAM BENJAMIN is a graduate of Brown University. He has worked variously as a farmhand, celebrity ghostwriter, massage therapist, and independent filmmaker. He is the author of *American Gangbang: A Love Story*, one of the *LA Weekly*'s Best Reads of 2011.

CANDICE LORI holds a BS in Philosophy and Religious Studies. She has spent the past decade studying yoga, organic horticulture, and bodywork at alternative communities in Hawaii, India, and California. She is currently a bodyworker and sacred dance space facilitator in Big Sur.

Acknowledgments

We'd like to thank the Rare Bird publishing team, Tyson Cornell, Alice Marsh-Elmer, and Julia Callahan for supporting our vision and giving us the opportunity to create this book; Tamryn Hawker, Kristen Parkhurst, and Grace Krilanovich for their creative counsel; Diem and Isis, for offering spontaneous inspiration; Sam Wohl for his unparalleled talent for bringing our ideas into form; and our friends and families, for their love and support on this journey.